Thriving and surviving at work

Disabled people's employment strategies

Alan Roulstone, Lorraine Gradwell, Jeni Price and Lesley Child

The POLICY PRESS

First published in Great Britain in July 2003 by

The Policy Press
Fourth Floor, Beacon House
Queen's Road
Bristol BS8 1QU
UK

Tel no   +44 (0)117 331 4054
Fax no   +44 (0)117 331 4093
E-mail   tpp-info@bristol.ac.uk
www.policypress.org.uk

Published for the Joseph Rowntree Foundation by The Policy Press

ISBN 1 86134 522 4

Alan Roulstone is currently Reader in Disability Policy in the School of Health, Natural and Social Sciences, University of Sunderland, **Lorraine Gradwell** is Chief Executive of Breakthrough UK Ltd, Manchester, a leading-edge social model organisation offering employment and independent living skills to disabled people, **Jeni Price** is founder of Equality Associates, Hove, a training and consultancy organisation specialising in disability equality issues and **Lesley Child** is a freelance Disability Equality Trainer based in the West Midlands.

The **Joseph Rowntree Foundation** has supported this project as part of its programme of research and innovative development projects, which it hopes will be of value to policy makers, practitioners and service users. The facts presented and views expressed in this report are, however, those of the authors and not necessarily those of the Foundation.

Cover design by Qube Design Associates, Bristol.
Printed in Great Britain by Hobbs the Printers Ltd, Southampton.

Contents

Notes on the research team

Alan Roulstone is Reader in Disability Policy at the University of Sunderland. He was previously Deputy Director of the Strathclyde Centre for Disability Research at the University of Glasgow. Alan has much experience of research on employment and social inclusion and has worked on Department for Education and Employment, European Commission and Economic and Social Research Council (ESRC) projects. He also provides consultancy and reviewing services for the Department of Health, ESRC and the Community Fund on disability-related issues. Alan's research is grounded in the social model of disability and draws on his own experiences as someone living with the social implications of an unseen impairment.

Lorraine Gradwell, Chief Executive of Breakthrough UK Ltd, was employed by Manchester City Council to set up the company and externalise employment services to it. She has had a long involvement with the disabled people's movement, primarily through the Greater Manchester Coalition of Disabled People, of which she is Deputy Chair, but also through such channels as the British Council of Disabled People and Unison structures regionally and nationally. With an MA in Disability Studies from Leeds University, Lorraine contributes to many 'mainstream' organisations and partnerships to promote the social model of disability as an approach to employment and, through that, to independent living.

Jeni Price is a freelance Disability Equality Consultant and Trainer. She has run her own business, Equality Associates, since 1996, which provides consultancy, training, research and writing on a range of disability equality issues. Jeni applies disability equality for employers, service providers and disabled people, working with organisations, companies and groups across the public, private, voluntary and trades unions sectors. Jeni has been involved in some key initiatives with disabled people on personal development, access and employment issues. As a disabled person, Jeni is active in a number of national and regional organisations of disabled people.

Lesley Child is a self-employed consultant, trainer and facilitator, her main specialism being disability equality. She has 20 years experience of paid work in local government, primarily in social work, equality, policy and quality. Lesley has been involved in training and consultancy since 1992. As an associate of a major consultancy organisation, she has undertaken work with a range of employers and service providers. As a disabled person, Lesley has also been actively involved with a wide range of local and national disability organisations. Lesley has served on the management committees of many of these disability organisations.

Acknowledgements

This research has been produced by
Breakthrough UK Ltd with the support,
both financial and practical, of the Joseph
Rowntree Foundation. The research team
is indebted to the hard work of the
Project Advisory Group. We would like
to thank Emma Stone for her assiduous
support as Project Manager and Dave
Cook, Dave Gibbs, Mark Hyde, Natalie
Markham, Tracy Proudlock and Lisa
Sutherland for their very helpful
comments and guidance on the research.
Thanks also to Rosalie Messina and Esther
Frank for their secretarial and
administrative support for the project.

To the participants in our research we are
particularly indebted; without their
enthusiasm and readiness to share their
experiences, this study would not have
been possible.

Thanks are also due to our interview
transcribers for the quality of their work,
their consistency and diligence.

Notes on the social model of disability

Disability has traditionally been defined in medical terms – an approach which focuses on the lack of physical, sensory or mental functioning and uses clinical terms to describe and label a disabled person. The emphasis is on cure or correction of the medical condition or impairment to what is perceived to be a 'normal' level of functioning. This approach has been described as a **medical model of disability**.

Disabled people have reinterpreted their own experience and many have found that it is more helpful to use an analysis based on an understanding of the barriers they encounter. This **social model of disability** does not deny the individual reality of impairment, but focuses on how environments, attitudes and institutional structures limit people with impairments.

In the context of work, a medical model approach would focus on rehabilitating the individual worker or jobseeker. From a social model perspective the focus is squarely on the physical, attitudinal and institutional barriers that limit workers with impairments and this is the model we have adopted in this study.

Executive summary

This work was based on interviews with 33 disabled workers, questionnaire responses from 156 people and two focus groups, in England, Wales and Scotland.

Employment strategies used

- Disabled workers used a diverse and often complex range of strategies to survive and/or thrive in the workplace. Key strategies included (in priority order):
  ‣ being assertive and direct
  ‣ openness about impairment, disability and barriers
  ‣ seeking external support (family, medical, benefits)
  ‣ use of new technologies to aid communication choices
  ‣ information management and targeting (impairment)
  ‣ seeking the validation of other disabled people
  ‣ seeking flexible working
  ‣ getting legal help
  ‣ personal development
  ‣ using impairment knowledge to get work
  ‣ gradual building up of strategies over time.

- There was no 'universal' strategy. What might work for one disabled worker may be unhelpful or risky for another, given the employment context, length of time in a given employment, the human resources and financial environment.
- The gradual introduction of strategies helped workers to survive and thrive, which can be viewed as a strategy in itself.
- Strategies changed over time as employment changed, management styles, personnel movements, corporate priorities and impairment changes occurred.
- The use of strategies was perceived by some to contain risks; for example, being too assertive or too sudden in asking for barriers to be removed.

The source and nature of support

- Workplace support, formal and informal, internal and external, was central to getting on at work for most disabled workers.
- Sources of support (in order of importance included:)

- colleagues
- the Employment Service
- family and friends
- employers and managers
- organisations of and for disabled people
- trades unions.

- Disabled workers employed in organisations of and for disabled people were more likely to receive substantial support in the workplace compared to those who did not. Greater levels of acceptance, flexibility and empathy were all commented on.

- A useful distinction was made between formal and informal support. Formal support was usually agreed in writing. Although coming from external and internal sources, this support would usually survive changes of personnel.

- Informal support was very important for many participants, and was based on understandings and arrangements that had emerged over some time. This form of support was based largely on friendship, altruism and mutual respect.

- Some forms of support did not fit clearly into these 'formal' and 'informal' categories. These may well have been established through workplace 'custom and practice' but not written down or known to a personnel department. The advent of the 1995 Disability Discrimination Act had mixed implications here: while some employers wanted to formalise these practices to avoid any uncertainties, there may have been a tendency to undermine the trust on which these arrangements were founded.

- **Informal support** was seen as very important to the majority of participants and took the following forms:
  - give and take about work
  - help and advice, guidance and material support
  - empathy, particularly in disability organisations.

- Support largely came at little financial cost to most disabled workers and reciprocal trade-offs were common. However, a small number of participants felt that there was an emotional cost attached to asking for support.

- **Formal Support** (in order of importance) included:
  - technological aids and equipment
  - changes to the work environment
  - flexible working (hours and location)
  - advice and welfare support
  - job redesign and reallocation
  - wage subsidies (for example through Workstep).

- The main source of support for workplace technology, environmental improvements, job design and reallocation was the Jobcentre Plus Access to Work scheme. Employer contributions were often also required.

- Minor or low-cost redesign, reallocation and work flexibility were often provided solely by the employer, with advice from Jobcentre Plus.

- A small number of participants reported using their trade union, human resources and/or welfare departments to begin the process of seeking formal support.

Stakeholder lessons

Messages for disabled workers

- Be open about impairment and barriers.
- Be assertive, not aggressive.
- Be aware of sources of aid and support.
- Be informed about rights at work.

Messages for employers, managers and colleagues

- Employers and managers should value diversity.
- Acknowledge disabled workers' strengths, not limitations.
- Build trust so that disabled employees feel able to voice their concerns.
- Be well informed about outside sources of support.
- Disability equality training for key staff should be a part of personal development at work.

Lessons for Jobcentre Plus staff

- Develop more awareness among disability service team frontline and management staff of the importance of the Access to Work scheme to many disabled workers in getting on at work.
- Be responsive and flexible to the needs of disabled workers.
- Be consistent and equitable in provision.
- Employ more disabled people in the application for and provision of Access to Work support.

Policy implications

- Greater awareness is needed of the importance of the Access to Work scheme in disabled workers' daily lives.
- Policies are needed to prevent the reported 'lottery' of provision being inflexible, slow, reactive provision and with a lack of specialist impairment knowledge.
- Much support that was of value to disabled workers is informal or derived from 'custom and practice', which makes some support time-limited and vulnerable to staff turnover.
- Statutory assumptions about the significance of personnel, welfare department, equal opportunities and trades unions support need to be revisited.
- Scandinavian and North American approaches to vocational support include the creative/cross-agency use of support and other professionals.
- Disabled workers' desire for more awareness by colleagues and managers about their use of strategies and support needs must be fed into employers, employer and personnel forums.
- Further consideration should be given to the role and scope of support that trades unions offer, as their members often saw them as a final option.
- Organisations of and for disabled people were seen to offer a more supportive environment for the workers employed by them.
- There were some clear messages from this research about developments in disability employment policy, especially on staying in work or keeping employees.

Surviving or thriving?

- A key message from the research was of the value, strength and resilience of the disabled people who took part in the study – many of whom had struggled with significant barriers to get to their current position. A significant minority, however, were still only surviving.
- Working for an organisation of and for disabled people was seen as far more likely to offer conditions in which disabled workers could thrive. Here diversity was seen as an asset, difference a source of validation and being a disabled person, a source of pride.

Most disabled participants were clear that they were thriving or surviving in the workplace, although a significant minority were getting on well in some aspects of their work but only surviving in others.

Background and context

Defining terms

This study took as its starting point the need to identify, analyse and disseminate the strategies and supports that enable workers with a range of impairments to get on at work. An important distinction was made between strategies and supports.

- **Strategies** stem from the individual disabled person. They involve thinking through options, making decisions and choices, planning ahead, working out the best ways to get by, taking action to get support in the workplace.
- **Support** comes from outside the individual: from a colleague, a scheme, financial allowances or benefits, or changes to the workplace. Support could be emotional, moral, practical, financial, technical, environmental or organisational. For a wider discussion of the definition of strategies and support see the Appendix.

This research revealed that workplace survival and success do not occur overnight. The complex relationships between disabled worker, colleagues, the changing work environment and role seniority, as well as discrimination or disadvantage and other personal or social characteristics needed to be understood.

Previous disability and employment research has noted the significance of impairment, its interaction with workplace barriers and facilitators. In this study, impairment was defined so as to include people with present or previous mental health problems and people with learning difficulties, as well as those with physical and sensory impairments. This did not compromise the social model focus of the study in identifying external barriers as the main limitation to workers with impairments. The research is clear, however, that the relationship between impairment, perceived impairment and workplace dynamics is very important and under-explored.

Context and aims of the study

This study was done in a response to identified and significant gaps in our understanding of disabled people's employment experiences. A review of research in the area of disability and employment (Barnes et al, 1998) identified significant gaps in our understanding of disabled people's daily employment experiences. Research on disabled people's employment and search for employment has concentrated on quantitative surveys of disabled people and employment (Martin et al, 1989), obtaining work (Lakey and Simpkins, 1994), mapping government support for disabled workers (Beinart et al, 1996) and latterly job and work retention (Lewis, 2000). There is little research exploring the daily experiences of disabled people at work.

Those qualitative studies which focused on the experience of employment have largely been based on the medical model of disability (Thomas, 1992). While those adopting a social model of disability have focused on a particular profession (French, 2001) or the impact of new workplace technologies on disabled workers (Roulstone, 1998).

Given the urgent need to improve disabled people's employment options and experience (Griffiths, 2001), this study aimed to go beyond a focus on workplace and labour market barriers. This research asked how working disabled people have managed to survive and thrive in the workplace. It is believed that many lessons can be learned by exploring the strategies and forms of support identified in disabled people's daily working lives. Personal, practice and policy insights can be gleaned from looking at a wide range of workplace strategies and support identified in disabled people's employment. However, it may only be possible to measure the real impact of disability employment policy and practice by exploring how disabled people's work,

employment practice and external policy provision interact.

This study aimed to respond to the limitations of previous research by grounding the research process and analysis in the social model of disability. Here the 'voices' of disabled people are central to the research and the findings. In addition, disabled workers are not seen as the research 'problem', instead, the contemporary organisation of the society and working life is seen as problematic. The following assumptions underlie this research:

- A range of different experiences were sought from a national profile of disabled workers to cover geographical, job status, employment type, ethnicity, impairment, gender, sexual identity and economic contexts.
- Disabled workers may remain in employment not solely because of externally directed policies and practices.
- The complex mix of policies designed to respond to disabled workers' needs are often contradictory and do not always enhance options for job retention and satisfaction.
- Disabled people are taking an active part in shaping their employment futures.
- Disabled workers are best able to identify factors that facilitate their employment.
- The interaction between worker and employer strategies is important.
- Wider support, whether formal or informal, is central to disabled workers surviving and thriving in their daily work.

- The voices of disabled people should be central to the research process and findings.

The policy environment

Recent research findings point to the barriers that continue to limit workers with impairments (Graham et al, 1990; Gooding, 1995; Burchardt, 2000; RNIB, 2002). These findings are vital to our understanding of the policy and practice changes required in the workplace. A parallel development is the growing activity geared to opening up the labour market to disabled jobseekers. This development draws on anti-discrimination and human rights discourses (Daw, 2000; DRC, 2002), the business case (Zadek and Scott-Parker, 2001) and managing workplace diversity (ILO, 2001). What these ideas have in common is the notion that many disabled people are employable and keen to work. The key obstacles to employment are therefore seen as the environmental, attitudinal, organisational and information/communication barriers that continue to undervalue and undermine disabled jobseekers.

The piloting and roll-out of the New Deal for Disabled People (NDDP) and the development of Jobcentre Plus symbolise the government's commitment to link more squarely the benefits system and the world of work (DfEE, 1998; DSS, 1999). The development of personal advisors and the ONE service (a single gateway to benefits, employment advice and support) are said to represent more joined-up responses to the work and welfare relationship, although interpretations do differ on the exact motivations of the NDDP (Roulstone, 2000). One obvious limitation of NDDP is that it does little to alter employer attitudes and behaviour; this in part explains why a recent government study established that only 30% of NDDP opportunity providers were achieving the targets set for them and only two providers were achieving targets nationally (*Disability Now*, 2002). This limited success rate may also be explained by the continued 'innovative' pilot status of NDDP, with an obvious and urgent need to mainstream the service. Of note, the North West consortium City Pride suggests that the New Deal should aim for 'parity of outcomes' for disabled people on the range of New Deal programmes. Also, the officially sponsored research evaluating NDDP notes the limited take-up rate by disabled people eligible for the programme (Sainsbury et al, 2001).

A potentially complementary policy development has been the advent of the 1995 Disability Discrimination Act (DDA). This Act has clearly been invested with much promise in its role of reducing discrimination in the workplace. Sadly, the evidence to date suggests that, despite a few landmark cases, the Act remains limited in the recruitment arena, is reactive, has failed to link legal interventions with the Access to Work scheme and offers a severe legal test very few disabled complainants can pass (Income Data Services, 2000; Roulstone, 2003: forthcoming). However, the actual workings of the DDA may be less important than the perception of the Act as a powerful tool in enforcing anti-discriminatory behaviour. It is important, therefore, that those 'high profile' cases that are of educational value to employers are broadcast as widely and deeply as possible. The Disability Rights Commission (DRC) could be more proactive in this regard. Policies on employment and social security must clearly run in parallel with legal developments if the benefits of both are to be realised. The connection between national policy shifts and the working of the Access to Work scheme requires particular attention given the reported benefits of the scheme in keeping disabled people in employment.

Despite these continued challenges to getting and keeping work, an important development is the increase in employer-led case study evidence and good practice in the employment of disabled people. The growth of the Employers Forum on Disability, the recent announcement of the work by Centrica (2001) in enhancing employment opportunities and the social model successes of Breakthrough UK (2001) all attest to recent high profile efforts to enhance disabled people's employment. These are very important developments and key lessons can be learned from these initiatives. We must be cautious, however, not to overlook the importance of unique organisational contexts and not to ignore the daily and often small-scale strategies and supports being used by disabled workers, their colleagues and managers. The failure to bring together important employer initiatives has contributed to a degree of policy muddle about lessons that can be learnt for disability and employment.

The most recent policy developments continue to emphasise the importance of paid employment as a key reference point for disabled people. Indeed, New Labour made an explicit commitment to this subject in its 1997 manifesto. In addition to the NDDP, job retention pilots and latterly job brokerage, the past two years have witnessed the introduction of the Workstep programme. Workstep represents a clear attempt to match

disabled workers to employment opportunities. It validates both supported employment (which is subsidised) and open employment (which is not) (DfEE, DSS and HM Treasury, 2001). The programme is underpinned by clear targets for participants' movement from supported employment into 'open employment'. A recent report expressed some concern that progression to open employment will be emphasised at all costs, which may work against some workers with learning difficulties (Jones et al, 2002) and visual impairments (RNIB, 2002).

New benefit-linking rules, an increased earnings disregard on Independent Living Fund payments, and broader shifts to welfare in work through work-based tax incentives all symbolise the government's commitment to disability employment policy. The *Valuing people* White Paper (DoH, 2001) – a major review of learning disability policy – makes explicit references to the need to reduce day centre provision in favour of open employment. Here, open employment is advocated for those who would benefit from it, while a carefully tailored subsidised employment would be offered to those for whom open employment presents too many barriers. The value of open employment for full market wages has been emphasised in recent commentaries drawing on North American notions of supported employment (O'Bryan et al, 2000). There is scope here for confusion between the two very different uses of the term 'supported employment'. Principles that have emerged largely from the US and Canada emphasise 'job matching', the identification of 'natural supports' and job coaches/mentors to help disabled employees perform a full range of employment tasks successfully and at the full market rate for the job. In the UK, supported employment has been based on employment subsidies. However, the recent development of Workstep may begin to break down this distinction as it attempts to borrow something from each tradition. Whether this works in practice is yet to be established.

The current policy emphases on job retention, anti-discriminatory practice and social inclusion through employment, work-based social benefits and the inclusive workplace need to be understood in the context of disabled people's working lives. The increasingly creative use of social policies to enhance disabled people's economic and social inclusion will only operate effectively when we understand how they are lived out in the workplace. It is also vital that current notions of capacity and incapacity are replaced with more enabling tools for connecting disabled people with the world of work (Bolderson and Mabbett, 2000). This study aims to begin the process of linking experiences, barriers, policy and practice in a meaningful way. This research was undertaken with the objective of learning lessons from disabled workers that can be passed on to key stakeholders: other disabled workers, employer organisations, trades unions, organisations of and for disabled people, and policy makers. The value of the study should be measured against the extent to which we have achieved this goal.

Outline of the methodology

This research was conducted throughout England, Wales and Scotland and aimed to maximise the range of employment experiences gleaned from disabled workers while retaining a depth of research findings. A three-phase methodology was adopted, which allowed for a large range of support and strategies to be mapped. Phase 1 was a questionnaire with 156 respondents. In Phase 2, 33 in-depth interviews were conducted, selected from Phase 1 respondents. In Phase 3, Phase 2 participants were invited to attend one of two focus group meetings (Manchester and London), where an outline of the research findings was presented. This was to verify and test the research findings.

Phases 1 and 2 of the research were piloted and every effort was made to provide alternative format questionnaires and appropriately designed interviews. Most interviews were undertaken by telephone. Where speech, hearing impairment or learning difficulties were an issue, face-to-face interviews were undertaken. Disabled people were fully consulted on the development of the research tools used. The research team all identify as disabled people, and members of the Project Advisory Group also represented a range of disability, impairment and employment issues and experiences from a range of perspectives. A more detailed examination of the research methodology is provided in the Appendix to this report.

Analysis of the questionnaire

In adopting a purposive sampling approach, it would be expected that the number of people citing the use of strategies and presence of supports would be high; this proved to be the case as all Phase 1 participants cited either strategies (95%) or support (75%) in their working lives. Women represented just over a half of respondents (58%).

Most respondents worked in larger organisations (60% in places employing more than a 101 employees), were based in urban employment (94%), had a physical or sensory impairment (70%) and worked in the public sector (62%). A north–south England spread of respondents was achieved, but only small numbers of respondents came from Wales or Scotland (4%). Most respondents worked full time (75%), although there was a significant minority of part-time workers.

The majority of respondents were clustered in the 35-54 age range (70%). 16% were under 35, which is significantly less than in the study of Access to Work recipients (Beinart et al, 1996), in which 36% were in this age group. Only 4% of respondents were from minority ethnic groups, which is roughly in line with the Access to Work research, but represents only six respondents. Caution is therefore required in drawing any general lessons, as more research would be required to explore the question of ethnicity, work strategies and support. The questionnaire included a question on sexual identity and asked participants (if they were willing to provide the information) if they considered themselves to be heterosexual, lesbian, gay, bisexual or 'other' in terms of their sexual identity. It was felt that this question was important since identification in one of these minority groups could impact on the experience of barriers and potentially any strategies used in the workplace. The researchers realised that such potentially complex layers of experience might provide additional insight into surviving and thriving in employment. In the event,

although 7% of participants identified in categories other than heterosexual, it did not form a significant or explicit issue within the in-depth interview findings.

Despite the best efforts of the research and advisory teams, the numbers of participants with learning difficulties (4%) and mental health problems (4%) was fewer than we had hoped for, although these figures are in line with other studies of disabled workers. The number of participants with mental health problems may be under-estimated, however. In one instance, mental health problems emerged in an interview with a participant who had not previously disclosed this information.

Few quantitative differences were found in terms of the numbers and types of employment strategies noted in relation to the variables identified. The use of strategies was not likely to be affected by size of organisation, employment sector, full- versus part-time working or gender.

In terms of support, however, women were more likely than men to cite sources of support. This needs to be interpreted carefully. It could indicate that men are slightly less likely to receive support generally. However, women may include expressions of friendship as part of their support. Women also cited more forms of support than did men but, again, this could be due to the definition of support. Whether the quality of support is seen to be different could only be discerned in the later qualitative findings.

Analysis of the interviews

For the 33 disabled workers interviewed in depth, getting on at work was a complicated process. Strategies varied from the most formal through to the very informal and low key. Support also ranged from that which was externally provided and monitored through to gradual and informal support. Sometimes this was the first time these issues had been thought about by the respondents. In some interviews people said that they found the discussion empowering and had encouraged them to perhaps ask for more support in future.

Phase 2 involved looking at possible gender factors in the receipt of support and strategies used. Women constituted 18 of the 33 interview participants (55%) and were more likely to cite support from their employer as important (10 women, 4 men). But women were also more likely to be working in organisations of or for disabled people (11 women, 2 men). This factor, rather than gender differences or gendered workspace, is likely to explain the greater likelihood of women receiving support. This is reinforced by the fact that there were no obvious gender differences in getting support from colleagues (11 women, 10 men).

The importance of the work context was seen as significant for disabled participants. A clear message coming from the interviews was that strategies and requests for support must be appropriate to the work environment. Clear risks were attached to more formal strategies and to requests for support. Workers said that they had generally become more confident over time as they gained experience in workplace self-management. The risks of asking for substantial support too early in employment, or of being over-enthusiastic about strategies adopted were clear.

Working in an organisation of or for disabled people generally provided an environment, both physical and relational, in which it proved easier to get on. Awareness of the social model of disability, or at least an acceptance of difference, characterised disability-related employment.

Working with other disabled people was another factor that influenced the range of support received at work. Other factors that improved the likelihood of getting on at work were being senior in an organisation and having autonomy over the working day. One often-overlooked fact about seniority emerged from the research: that of a reluctance to ask for informal support. It may be assumed that being at or near the top of an organisation means that everything is sorted out but, while formal supports can be arranged by the use of power at work, it is arguably more difficult to get the reciprocal support that others may receive from colleagues.

The overall relationship between surviving and thriving is a complex one. Workers in disability-related work felt that they undertook highly rewarding work that validated and enhanced disabled people's self-worth in and beyond their employment. In this sense, thriving did not mean the absence of the workplace problems (which most workers might face), but rather satisfying work where the dynamics of disability did not dominate daily working life.

Survival as defined by disabled workers was a little more difficult to define but included workers encountering continued barriers in the workplace, but who had developed strategies and received supports that made work possible.

However, a small number of respondents
felt that they thrived as valued colleagues,
but only survived financially because their
benefit–work conditions were very
restrictive. This detail suggested that a
simplistic use of the terms 'thrive' and
'survive' as global definitions of workers'
experiences needed to be avoided.

The following chapters explore in depth
the strategies used and support cited by
disabled workers. Strategies and supports
are presented as separate chapters of the
report for clarity, each beginning with a
summary of the strategies and supports
cited.

2

Disabled workers' employment strategies

Exploring strategies

This chapter covers the following strategies:

- being assertive and direct
- being open
- seeking external support
- using information and communications technologies
- managing personal information
- seeking the validation of other disabled people
- flexible working
- 'getting legal' (adopting formal or legal strategies)
- personal development
- using disability experience to gain supportive work.

Being assertive and direct

The most commonly used strategy was being assertive and clear about impairment, its effects, disability and barriers. Being direct, confident and assertive early on was seen as important by many disabled workers in getting changes at work, resolving access issues and being accepted as a colleague. This approach was often used early in employment. Being direct showed itself in different ways. Katherine requested Access to Work support before starting her present job; she made it clear that she could not begin the job in question without this support. She also suggests that planning ahead and working cooperatively are part of her strategy of being direct:

> "Well, yeah I suppose to say 'look, I need equipment' before I even start a job and that's always been a thing ... I think that was a two-way thing, because of who they are – the Northern Disability Forum – they knew they had to do it anyhow and I knew from the last time I couldn't start a job without it [Access to Work support]. It was definitely a joint thing." (Katherine)

Katherine's direct approach was well received and she made it clear that the employer has a high degree of disability awareness. Marge was also direct in emphasising her needs as a worker with dyslexia, but admitted to some difficulty in sustaining this approach:

> "Well I made it very clear that these aren't trivial things and I'm very, very forward in demanding

other people's access needs being met, but it's very difficult when its you.... I do have needs and if these things aren't here I cannot do my job." (Marge)

Being direct requires assertiveness and confidence. Here, Ruth conveys the general need to assert her rights as a disabled worker:

"... there is a danger of the disabled person or woman or black person ending up the passive victim of other people's racial harassment or sexism or anti-disability attitudes.... I believe very strongly that part of what disabled people have to do is empower ourselves. Equality is never going to be given to us, we have to assert it in a way that is positive, to be assertive and not aggressive."
(Ruth)

Being direct and assertive may involve rejecting opportunities that are seen to be inappropriate:

"Oh yes, because at the time of my appraisals she [manager] did actually ask me if I wanted to become a property manager and I said 'no'. And the reason I said 'no' was not the administration work or the phoning people, but because you had to go round and out and visit the properties, which was not a practical thing for me to do." (Joanne)

Being direct was not always synonymous with being in the 'driving seat'. Ruth made clear her dislike of dealing with Jobcentre Plus staff, saying that she preferred her manager to deal with them. This understanding of 'direct' is similar to

the use of the term 'independence' to mean choice, rather than doing everything for yourself.

"... there is a basic patronisation and a basic attitude that we should be grateful – I should be grateful. The meetings that I have to have with Access to Work people I find insufferable, absolutely insufferable. As far as I possibly can I avoid it and just leave my manager or anyone I can find to deal with Access to Work." (Ruth)

For Mary assertiveness was not caring what other people thought of her hearing impairment:

"... I think that part of my personal development was around caring less about whether other people didn't like it or not and feeling more confident about the fact that I had a right to participate in something." (Mary)

Josh provided an example of how he used his impairment knowledge to take control of new workplace encounters:

"... for example, on one occasion I actually said 'now don't worry about visual impairment, I'm the expert there, I'm in control, I'm in charge, if you have got any worries I will sort them out with you, you know the job here, I know my disability, so feel relaxed'." (Josh)

Being open

Another key strategy adopted by disabled workers was that of openness. More participants felt it important to be open than to conceal issues. It was seen as important by some workers to be up-front about impairment and disability issues:

> "... I think it helps if you work with the same people obviously for a long time. Most of the people are very good if you explain to them what the problem is, then I think part of the strategy you should adopt is to talk to people.... I've got one work colleague who's been working with me for years now, she's very good, helping me, she understands the problems." (James)

It is worth noting that the scope for openness is greater in established jobs where there is already trust. Sheila emphasised the need to select, where possible, an organisation where she could be open about her mental health problems and feel free to be perhaps more open and honest than elsewhere:

> "... I couldn't work in a job where I wasn't accepted for what I am ... because of my limitations or vulnerabilities, whatever you want to call them, I have to be able to be honest about the fact that ... I don't always handle things 100% well, but I do have a mental health history ... sometimes I need things that are not conventional. For instance there is an issue with flexi-work at the moment, which is very difficult, so because of that I need to work in a field where I can be open and honest." (Sheila)

Workers with learning difficulties who had significant barriers at work said that being open about their learning needs and asking questions was important. Mike commented on the benefits of being

open about his needs as a worker with dyslexia:

> "Yes, I had to ask that person for ... I asked that colleague for help because it's difficult for other people to know what's going on in my mind.... It's informal in that I can ask anybody who is free to answer that question." (Mike)

Another worker with dyslexia, Keith, found that coming to terms with his specific learning difficulty led to an assessment that provided an explanation of his problems in handling information in written form. This process provided Keith and his colleagues with clear ideas about the best way to manage and support his work.

Seeking external support

The full range of advice, support and guidance was not seen as coming from within the workplace. Despite evidence of supportive employers (many of whom had sound welfare and equal opportunities policies and procedures in place), a number of disabled workers also looked for external sources of advice and help. Strategies ranged from drawing on moral support from family and friends to asking employers to call on expert ergonomic, medical and psychological advice, including from Jobcentre Plus. The search for support from family and friends was commented on by Mary (a worker with a hearing impairment):

> "I have always needed to have ... not exactly deaf support ... but it acknowledges that in me ... I have always managed to find a group of people, or it might be at home – partners, friends who actually

nourish me as a whole person – and that has been quite an important strategy." (Mary)

Alicia reflected on how, in her last job, she had sought advice when an office move provided an opportunity to respond to her ergonomic (workspace design and layout) needs. Alicia called on her employer and eventually the local Disability Support Team to assess her needs as a worker with right-sided hemiplegia:

> "... I said to them 'I need an office to be laid out left-handed' ... they all said 'we've seen a difference in the way that you are doing things now', and to me that was just commonsense type of attitude." (Alicia)

Walter also provided an account of a specific use of outside expertise. He related how the fear of being retired early led him to seek a second medical opinion. It is clear from Walter's wider comments that he would have been retired from his previous job had he not sought this opinion:

> "... I was having to take so much time off with the circulation problem, I went to see a specialist at the hospital who said he can't see why I cannot go back to work. It was my doctor who was stopping me going back to work – I had to override him." (Walter)

Ahmed provided an unusual and creative example of a way of gaining support for himself as a self-employed business owner with a hearing impairment. He related how an awareness of the limited availability of sign language interpreters led to his setting up a short course to teach British Sign Language to provide him with an enlarged 'pool' of interpreters:

> "The interpreters were very busy and, yes, you are right, it was a little bit risky [becoming self-employed]. That's why I decided to teach sign language so I could create more interpreters, because everyone who is deaf needs an interpreter for them." (Ahmed)

Using information and communications technologies

A number of workers said how hardware and software developments allowed them communication choices that would not have been previously available. The use of information and communications technologies was seen as improving working lives for some disabled workers. This did not just refer to new computerised workplace technologies but also to 'old' technologies such as phones and faxes. Strategies varied, with some workers choosing certain technologies, others deciding not to in order to encourage better forms of communication in their work. Mary, a worker with a hearing impairment, noted:

> "I make great use of fax and minicom; I have a uniphone at work and email.... Sometimes I don't put my phone number on [letters and faxes], I just put the fax number on and on my fax I have a message which says: 'this telephone receives fax calls only, please fax on this number', or something like that." (Mary)

Both Alan and Josh noticed that they used certain technologies more than their colleagues. Alan, who has cerebral palsy, chose to use email more than speech-based technologies, while Josh, a worker with a visual impairment, preferred using the telephone to face-to-face communication:

> "I use the telephone more than other people do ... maybe it actually puts me at a slight advantage ... I don't always pick up on conversational cues and therefore I will leap in. But on the telephone we are very much working on audio cues and therefore that evens things out."
> (Josh)

Managing personal information

A small number of disabled workers felt that in less inclusive organisations, rather than being open about impairment, disability and workplace barriers, they needed to hide or manage information about themselves. Complex layers of revealing information were shown. Henry related how he had become more confident over time, but that his work history revealed his efforts to play down the impairment effects of polio:

> "I would straighten up and make sure I was walking properly without a limp ... the limp is a natural thing for me and I didn't want to appear before managers and them saying 'oh why is he limping?'" (Henry)

Pauline made specific comparisons between her current and previous jobs and noted how she was now much more likely to feel able to be open with her employers:

> "I think if I was having difficulty doing my job because of my impairment I'd be more likely to tell my current employers than I would have done in the past. It's a different environment, they understand the problems I have, whereas at 'Phonecoms', there were very few people there in the department I worked in and you were expected to just cope."
> (Pauline)

Jack, successfully self-employed, made a more general comment about managing personal information. Despite feeling that his previous job as a lecturer in physiotherapy was not well supported, he felt it was better to not make an issue of the barriers that he faced. This is a major contrast to the above discussion about being open and assertive. Clearly the employment context is important in deciding which strategy or strategies to adopt.

> "Well basically [my strategy was] to keep a low profile. I suppose and I only asked for something when I absolutely needed anything.... Physiotherapists like I was are very alarmed by disability and they basically don't want to know."
> (Jack)

In contrast to the use of the early and direct strategies highlighted above, a small number of disabled workers felt it was better for them to adopt a gradual but planned strategy. This approach may not be very different to that noted earlier in the comments about directness not working in all contexts. Trevor provided an example of this gradual approach:

"Well, if I was starting a new job I think I'd try to be as independent as I could for a start, however hard it was. Then I think people would start offering to do things for you if they can see the things you are struggling with, or if you actually have to ask 'would you mind doing this for me?', then I think that would probably find its own level." (Trevor)

Seeking the validation of other disabled people

Contact with other disabled people – both individuals and organisations – was seen as helpful for advice, support and strategies at work, particularly in a new job or work role. There were ways of sharing stories and insights, which validated their identity as a disabled person and in some instances provided a forum where problems could be discussed or even overcome.

Caroline related her strategy of seeking support among established disabled friends and acquaintances in order to help both her job and moving towns:

"I was away for a couple of years and then moved back and I sort of met up with other disabled people – one person in particular who became a good friend. She was one of the first people here to sort of fight for and achieve her rights to the Independent Living Fund and stuff like that, and I suppose she was a bit of an inspiration." (Caroline)

Anwar made a similar point and, although he continued to face barriers at work, he felt that being able to talk these through with other disabled people was important:

"... there were a couple of other members of staff who were disabled who you would talk to over lunch and discuss your common problems and pretty much you always felt there wasn't anything you could do about it, but at least you could talk to people about it." (Anwar)

Jack noted how trying to gain solidarity through a formal staff group of disabled people led to a much wider organisational strategy for disabled people:

"I took over the Chair of the Principal's Advisory Group on Disability and ... I found a whole number of people in the university who recognised the inequalities of different situations and we worked together to develop strategies, overall for the university, and actually they worked very well." (Jack)

Flexible working

Although evidence of part-time, pro-rata and portfolio working featured in the research and were seen to be supportive, there was little evidence of a strategic or planned use of these forms of working. Flexible hours and working in different places was important for those workers whose impairments changed over time. It took the following forms: asking for leeway as to when particular tasks were completed, being able to go home early on a given day, minor job reallocation or working in a seasonal way when this was not usual for the job in question. Kate provided an example of a minor reallocation of her employment:

> "They've [managers] redesigned the branch and it meant high chairs and it does put a bit of strain on me physically ... so I've only had a limited time serving on the tills to really reduce additional strain in that respect." (Kate)

Libby discussed how she strategically took annual leave and unpaid leave for a large part of the year to allow her to recuperate or manage 'flare ups' with her impairment:

> "I negotiated over the last few years a period of annual leave which means I work for eight months of the year and take two months annual leave. I would take holidays either side of the unpaid leave to pump up those bits of time and I've done that for two years now." (Libby)

Lyn works in disability arts and has a learning difficulty. She noted how colleagues responded to her requests for assistance by being flexible in helping her learn and complete what she considered to be difficult tasks:

> "Sometimes I'm not very good at writing it [the agenda] out so I get Jack to do that on the computer, and he puts pictures on it as well so they can understand, 'cause people prefer pictures because it gets the message across." (Lyn)

'Getting legal'

A small number of disabled workers used the 1995 Disability Discrimination Act to

strategic effect. This did not involve submission to a tribunal, or the taking of legal advice, but rather letting an employer know that the disabled worker was aware of the Act's existence. This was significant as it may have a leverage effect on an employer's response and it is less risky than actively resorting to legal action.

Ahmed told how in a previous job he had threatened the Employment Service with legal action if he wasn't provided with Access to Work support. This is noteworthy, as the exact relationship between the Act's requirements and operation of the Access to Work scheme remains unclear.

> "I remember 11 years ago there was a thing called DRO [disablement resettlement officer] at that time ... I asked them for an interpreter but they refused. Then there was PACT [Placing, Assessment and Counselling Team], and this time I asked again for an interpreter and they refused again. And then the DDA [Disability Discrimination Act] started in '95 and I asked them for an interpreter and they refused. Then they agreed to give me an interpreter ... in '97. I said that if they refused again I would take them to court because I wanted to fight for my rights." (Ahmed)

Kate provided an interesting example of how a worker can be aware of disability law, make efforts to discover what her rights are, but use informal methods with her employer, keeping legal action as a fallback option:

> "I've used the staff union as a guide really as to how they felt it

[increased hours] should be approached.... Sometimes it works better if you are doing things on an informal basis, even if you personally have a strategy behind that, asking for that so that other things fall into place. You might not want them to be aware that you've calculated that so carefully." (Kate)

Personal development

Although many allusions were made in the interviews to education and training, only three disabled workers referred to them as strategies. Personal development was viewed as a strategic move in the following comment from Kate:

"... you could say that any qualification or continuance of education is important if you're going into a job, whatever job it is, because the learning continues even if it's not formally.... I mean, whatever perspective this learning goes on in, if you can show you are continuing your education, keen to learn, keen to take on new things, that, in an employment situation, is well received." (Kate)

Using disability experience to gain supportive work

Working in an organisation that uses the experience and awareness of disability was useful to a small number of disabled workers in helping them to thrive at work. Mary chose to work in an organisation for Deaf people (capital 'D' here denotes a Deaf identity, not simply having a hearing impairment). She felt well qualified to do this kind of work,

while she also received validation from the work as someone with a hearing impairment:

"... I have spent all my working life in what you might call a hearing world ... I wanted to work in the field of Deafness. Yes, I think it probably was because of my own impairment ... I think it was about acknowledging there is valid expertise that I have picked up because I am Deaf." (Mary)

Mike offered a slightly different take on the relationship between impairment and the work he does. Issues of identity as a disabled person were important for Mike and in seeking out disability-related work he realised that he would like to work in the field of disability arts. He felt this offered experiences that he could relate to as someone with a learning difficulty. It also showed the value of voluntary work as a graduated path to (supported) employment.

"I think it was a bit of an accident that I started work for an organisation of people with learning difficulties. I went to a northern town in 1997, as we saw the organisation working, doing a presentation and I was very impressed by the way it put very hard ideas across using very simple language.... I had an interview with Helen, who was the director ... I worked as a volunteer for about two years and then some money became available for me to be paid for the type of work that I was already doing." (Mike)

Risks of adopting strategies

There are risks in adopting certain strategies at given times and in particular work contexts, and a number of workers felt it was important to make judgements or take a 'reading' of an organisation before deciding on appropriate strategies. These judgements could be seen as strategies themselves of course. Ruth related how she decided to return to employment after a period of illness. She had previously had significant workplace support, but felt that she was taking a big risk in entering a new job with old assumptions. Here, risk was attached to job change, where a strategy of returning to work risked falling flat because of poor levels of ongoing support:

> "... in some senses I did take a very big risk that I could end up in a job where I wouldn't get that [previous] level of support." (Ruth)

Ruth adopted strategies to reduce these risks. Alison who has dyslexia made a similar point about the risks of assuming levels of support in the wider organisation:

> "It is very easy to get lost in an organisation like that because it is very protective and obviously you have a huge contact with outside society and all the issues involved. But in terms of reality and dealing with other employers, the support out there is nothing to what I received from my staff team and from the management team." (Alison)

Mary made a more general observation about the risks of disabled people being assertive in the workplace:

> "It is very easy if you are a disabled person to get labelled as having a 'chip on your shoulder', even if you haven't, if you are the slightest bit over the top about your needs." (Mary)

Walter sounded a similar note of caution about the use of strategies:

> "Yes, you have to be careful that you don't overuse them; you don't pressurise people, that you don't go on and on." (Walter)

Keith made a more specific point about the decision to reduce the total working hours:

> "I mean, some people can lose self-esteem in working less hours by feeling that they aren't contributing, so I think that you have to be careful on that one.... In some [work] cultures it would be very much frowned upon. Because we are talking about a generally feminine environment, its not so much of an issue if somebody works part time." (Keith)

There may be an important message here about men having less strategies available to them with regard to the length of their working week. This is a preliminary observation that needs further research.

Libby reflected on the limits of the openness strategy she otherwise adopted with her employers:

> "Well I suppose what I'm saying is, about the honesty thing, it actually goes up to a point and it's kind of hard to explain really, but it's like I'll be honest unless I think it

means I'm going to be discriminated against and then I will clam up and be more careful about what I say ... so I might not be honest about what's going on in terms of a flare up."(Libby)

Matthew pointed out the benefits of timing major employment strategies:

"Well, if you take risks at the beginning of your career you have everything to gain by them succeeding and not much to lose. At the end of your career you've got nothing to lose as it were. It's only in the middle of your career where there may be more to lose from taking the risk than there is to gain from taking the risk." (Matthew)

The inherent risk of using strategies per se was mentioned by one participant who chose not to use them:

"It's difficult to talk about strategies, I don't see my life in such a calculated way. If you were to do that, everything would fall apart." (Alan)

This is obviously a minority view and it is worth noting that Alan had received significant workplace support and used his trade union to change things. However, he made the point that some workers may feel that the timing for adopting strategies is risky for other relationships at work.

Conclusions

Many diverse strategies are used by disabled people at work. Some disabled workers adopted more than one strategy at a time, most notably openness about impairment and disability, and assertiveness about their needs at work. Other workers developed strategies gradually, preferring to play down their needs at first, but became more confident over time. The speed and stridency of using strategies depended much more on the nature and culture of the workplace for some workers than it did for others.

Clearly, some strategies contrasted with others, for example directness and assertiveness with a gradual approach or 'keeping your head down' as ways of surviving or thriving at work. It is important to note that directness was no guarantee that the person would be thriving in the workplace rather than surviving. Conversely, keeping a low profile could provide a more congenial climate for working with line managers, while being more likely to keep barriers in place.

Directness and openness, the most commonly mentioned strategies, were universally applied. The length of time in employment, the workplace culture, employer attitudes, disabled workers' awareness of their rights and awareness of a range of support were all important factors in predicting the kind of strategies used.

3

Support and disabled workers

Disabled workers used a wide range of support for surviving or thriving at work. Support was seen to come from both internal and external sources and to be formal (written) or informal. The terms 'formal' and 'informal' were found to be essential to understanding the different categories of support. However, this was not always clear-cut. A number of what might appear to be informal types of support were well established through custom and practice, and apparently formal support may simply have emerged and developed over time.

As with strategies, supports may have their origins in earlier personal experiences, or be recent and current forms of support. The study showed that family and educational influences and pre-employment factors generally were of significance when understanding the role and nature of support.

Overall, the most commonly cited sources of support (highest first) were:

- colleagues (21/33)
- Jobcentre Plus/Access to Work (18/33)
- family and friends (15/33)
- employer/manager (12/33)

- organisations of and for disabled people (11/33)
- trades unions (3/33).

As with strategies, women were slightly more likely than men to acknowledge the use of support and to use multiple forms of support. Although no clear or conclusive gender explanations emerged, the most likely reason for this continued difference is that women are significantly more likely to be working in an organisation of or for disabled people where the greatest range and depth of support was noted. That is, gender appears to influence work in an organisation of or for disabled people.

The differences in levels of support for men and women applied only to employers and managers, with 10 women (from 18) and 4 men (from 15) mentioning this source of support. There were virtually no gender differences in the sources of support received from colleagues (11 women, 10 men). There was a slight difference in those reporting support from family and friends (9 women, 6 men).

Informal support

Informal support was usually unwritten and not formally evaluated. It was defined as those forms or support that were not written or codified, including family, friends, colleagues, organisations of or for disabled people, employers/managers and other disabled people.

This chapter particularly examines:

- moral and financial support
- empathy and accepting difference
- 'give and take'.

Moral and financial support

Moral and financial support was provided to disabled workers mainly by family and friends, and less so by organisations of/for disabled people and colleagues. This support often emerged in an unplanned way but was significant in workers' daily lives.

The public nature of work and its distance from family life could make it easy to under-estimate its importance in providing moral and material support. This support was noted before and after starting work, and in a variety of jobs. Walter noted how, despite childhood impairment, his mother encouraged him:

> "Well my mum ... she said 'it's your life, you run it as you want it'. I was born without a thyroid gland so I have lived on tablets all my life.... She [mother] didn't mollycoddle me, she said 'go and get it, get on with it'. You cannot be shielded from everything, you have got to get on with it like everyone else." (Walter)

Joanne made similar comments about her parents' emphasis on avoiding 'special' treatment:

> "Well, I have always worked. When I left boarding school I came home and went to commercial college, I got qualifications there and my parents said 'it's entirely up to you'.... And it never, to be honest, occurred to me not to go out to work – all my friends worked, all my parents' friends worked – it was the normal thing to do." (Joanne)

Joanne went on to say how the encouragement to go to college and go out to work also made her willing to take risks and to try new challenges:

> "... you just have to be willing to try new things which is something they [line managers] always say in my appraisals – that I am always wanting to have a go at things, even if I have not done it before." (Joanne)

Similarly, Libby said:

> "... I missed chunks of time because I was having surgery and there was a further time where I wore a calliper, but there were other times when I was quite active and I was playing football and running around. Yes, I was limping, but ... my mum's attitude was always 'I wanted her to be treated like other kids'." (Libby)

This support was important before going to work; it was also useful to some people in their current work. Sharon commented:

"I think they have a good understanding of the job that I have … that I want to come home and offload sometimes and that I am tired, ratty, in pain, whatever it is, and they don't mind … and also that family and friends sometimes have also said to me 'well, if you need anything doing as well just give me a ring'." (Sharon)

Mike, an arts worker with a learning difficulty, got financial support from his father to help him buy a computer, which has allowed him to become more confident with new technologies. This has helped him at work.

"[My father] gives me a certain amount each month … it is regular and he's also very generously paid for a computer that I now use … at home, because it was clear that I had to learn how to use a computer here for the work that I do here. So it was to help me with the work here and to help me gain more confidence using a computer generally." (Mike)

Empathy and accepting difference

A key form of validation for disabled workers was that of working in organisations of and for disabled people with wider 'exposure' to ideas about the social model of disability. This was especially prevalent in organisations with a number of disabled workers, who were willing to share ideas in a supportive way. Alicia, who worked in an organisation of disabled people, highlights the value of this in giving her a new perspective on disability and her experience:

"… the first time I discovered the social model was when I was researching my dissertation in my final year of the university … I just sort of remember reading about the social model and thinking 'yeah, that's how I'd love it, that's me'. You know, it fitted in with everything I'd ever thought about disability, you know, in terms of the fact that if I'm not able to do something and it's other people preventing me from doing that then I've always thought 'well, that's their problem'." (Alicia)

Jack makes a similar point about an organisation of disabled people:

"Everybody said that the organisation was definitely needed and the reason it's needed is for solidarity. Basically, as individuals it's very easy for society to put us down, and it's only when we are together working collectively that actually we get the strength to say 'no, that isn't reasonable'." (Jack)

The value of solidarity and shared identity is clear in Lyn's experience of belonging to an organisation for people with learning difficulties:

"Well, I used to go before I started working. I used to go to a Friday club and that was made up of disabled people … we shared our experiences with and got a lot of information from other people.… They helped me build my confidence up; they helped me speak up for myself." (Lyn)

Sometimes support was more practical advice and help, as Alison pointed out:

"Some things from Access Rights [organisation of disabled people], which I have taken from there, is basically a lot of stuff around law – people have rights; you don't have to accept second best.... And the practical experience of working in an organisation where I could put out my needs and know my needs were heard and, most of all, valued." (Alison)

Caroline reinforced this view:

"The support that comes from fellow disabled colleagues who I kind of identify with, where I am coming from in terms of politics and the social model and stuff. So that kind of moral support, I suppose; having to argue about the finer points of language, some of 'Rangefinder' [non-disabled] employees have less awareness of language and stuff." (Caroline)

Similarly, for Lyn, a worker with learning difficulties:

"Advance [organisation for people with learning difficulties] can actually support people and help people to fight for their rights as well, and not just in Advance, but all people with learning disabilities.... Maybe we go to conferences, and we do a lot of campaigning as well." (Lyn)

Alison, who has dyslexia, faced challenges at work about the written word (documentation, signs); she talked about her previous work in an organisation of disabled people. She has been able to use these ideas and experiences in her current work. In concrete terms she gets help to access and inform people.

"I try to use a dictionary, but for a dictionary you need to able to visually see the words ... so I ask people how to spell, I say to people 'I am going to ask you words, if you've any difficulty with it just let me know'.... I talk a lot about dyslexia and about disability, most people are quite interested when they find out – 'oh, is that dyslexia?' – so some people are very receptive to that." (Alison)

'Give and take'

One key type of informal support reported was that of 'give and take' in working with colleagues and managers. Reciprocal arrangements usually took the form of informal arrangements with colleagues providing mutual support in the workplace. For many workers, being able to reshape the working day allowed them to work most effectively. This was especially significant when energy and pain levels might change according to work routines and rigid timetables. Peter gave a useful example of this informal but pivotal flexibility. Such support from colleagues usually carried little or no cost to the disabled person, although a small number of workers mentioned the emotional or personal costs of receiving help and support.

Peter commented:

"I developed a condition ... the result of this has left me in pain down my right side and my right arm, and to quell the pain I take more stringent drugs, which can result in very sudden bouts of drowsiness that I need to manage. If I wasn't in a sympathetic and empathetic environment I wouldn't feel comfortable. So that makes a two-way relationship – they give me a lot and then I feel I have to give them a lot. And I'm, in a way, bonded more to the people I work with now than I've been to anybody else." (Peter)

Walter, a public building assistant, also commented on this:

"… if they think I shouldn't be climbing stairs they will keep me on the ground floor. Normally they will either cut that floor out there or I will sweep the [entrance] steps. If they pick up on that I'm not feeling 100% they'll say 'take your time, do what you want to do, you don't have to knock yourself out'." (Walter)

Peter and Walter raised the significance of informal, flexible working with their non-disabled colleagues and managers. An example of a supportive workplace was also provided by Alicia, who works in a place in which all her colleagues are disabled people:

"The way that we work it is that we've all got very different impairments and different strengths and weaknesses in the office. So, for example, our use of the filing cabinet is quite creative in that I can't reach the bottom drawer of the filing cabinet and my colleague's a wheelchair user so he cannot reach the top, but my other colleague can, so myself and my wheelchair-using colleague will use the middle two drawers

because that's the level we can access." (Alicia)

This very simple agreed solution to barriers shows the ease with which adjustments can be made, but also reflects a supportive workplace. Physical environments sometimes reflect wider attitudes rooted in the social model of disability.

Trevor commented on informal support:

"Somebody – one of the members of staff – they help me transfer from my car into my wheelchair and at the end of the day it's the other way around…. Oh, and things like having a cup of tea. I can't get into the canteen because there's so many doors (well, even if I got in I wouldn't get out again with a cup of tea in my hand and that would be dangerous), so one of the chaps [a colleague] makes a cup of tea twice a day." (Trevor)

Support can extend to beyond the workplace. Gordon described how colleagues help him access council documents otherwise not available to him as a worker with a visual impairment and epilepsy:

"Members of staff, they say they'll always support me. All I have to do is go and have a chat with them. Just what I need. For example, I'm thinking of going to get a council flat so I am just going to ask them about what the council's procedure is." (Gordon)

For some employees the knowledge that further support would be available helped in itself. The prospect of future support, should it be needed, gave workers confidence so that they could continue to thrive in their work. Anwar discusses this point:

> "... if you do go to them [management] I'm pretty sure that they would take it seriously and be ok with any suggestions that you make, whether that be support in the sense that you have different hours of work or one day at home or whatever." (Anwar)

It is clear from Anwar's comment that, although not using these strategies, he is reassured that his work could be altered should it need to be.

Sheila has a physical impairment and mental health issues, and talks about how her manager and colleagues are at the heart of her workplace support:

> "I think I need an atmosphere of trust. Where I will give my best ... people accept me for who I am I suppose, with vulnerabilities more ... and it is when somebody accepts that you can be weak, that you can be your most strong, which is personal, but it does have a professional application." (Sheila)

Some participants felt that the research process was itself a supportive learning process in asking participants to reflect on these strategies. For example, Mary stated:

> "I think the questionnaire probably triggered it off and made me think, as so often things do. If you have to explain to somebody how you pick out the bits that you put together to make your strategy ... and maybe before that I wouldn't

have called it a strategy – it was just the way I did things." (Mary)

Pauline made a similar point:

> "Yes, I think that's the one thing really, perhaps I've done that without realising it is a strategy to improve the sort of work I'm doing." (Pauline)

Formal support

Although the boundaries were not always clear, distinctions were made between formal and informal support. Formal support was written down and used by disabled workers more generally. Formal support came from employers and managers, Jobcentre Plus (mostly through the Access to Work programme) and occasionally from welfare, personnel departments and trades unions. It took the form of aids, equipment and advice (largely under the Access to Work scheme, although some employers did provide smaller packages of support), and formalised arrangements for flexible work and the reallocation of work roles.

Access to Work

The Access to Work scheme clearly played a significant role in supporting over half of the disabled workers interviewed, although experiences of Access to Work's effectiveness varied widely. Perhaps surprisingly, trades unions, welfare officers, equal opportunities staff and personnel managers featured far less in disabled workers' comments.

Jobcentre Plus was seen by many as providing a wide variety of workplace support. This ranged from advice and assessment to ergonomic adjustments, 'Fares to Work' and complex technological support. Most provision was made under the Access to Work scheme, which funds environmental, technological, personal and travel to work support.

Sharon used different methods to make work more accessible:

> "I did have an occupational therapist come out and check desk heights, chairs, how the computer was situated, and she gave me advice and information on how to use things: foot rests and chairs and how to place the computer.... And they also help with travel costs for myself and that's continued for three years." (Sharon)

Although it took a year, Marge felt that new technology provided through Access to Work had supported her dyslexia:

> "They [Employment Service] came up with some extra stuff that I didn't know exists, like a dictaphone that plugs into my voice dictate thing [speech activated software] ... so, if I'm at a meeting and I need to take notes ... I can talk to a machine. I needed a palmtop because I use my diary here on my computer and they've been supportive of that, so I couldn't have done it without them." (Marge)

Similar creative solutions to workplace barriers were mentioned by Matthew, whose employer and the Employment Service PACT team (now Jobcentre Plus and the Disability Services Team) worked together to make the workplace more suited to his needs:

> "For example, the office that I have at the moment had sash windows in it, which I can't use and the university has replaced them with a window which opens and closes. It collaborates with the Access to Work people quite well. They've provided me with the computer that I use at home. Oh, and the university has provided me with a laptop computer that I use in my teaching...." (Matthew)

Ruth, a worker with a hearing impairment, received a wide-ranging package of support through the Access to Work scheme. Although unhappy about the process of getting support, Ruth clearly saw the benefits of having more access to the spoken word in her working environment:

> "Well, if I can start with the basics, I use hearing aids, which gives me a great deal of access to sound – a limited amount to be able to distinguish language; I then have a portable induction loop system, which is very expensive but it's what works for me ... in very formal meetings I have someone who goes round – a microphone mover placing it in front of whoever is speaking. It's very hard for me to be taking notes and be in a meeting, so if I need a note-taker they can do that; they will provide me with that." (Ruth)

Sheila gave an example of unusual help from Access to Work funds: she was provided with financial help with dealing with the challenges of her work:

> "I have had the support from Access to Work in getting a therapist to help me deal with things that I find very challenging and also travel to work costs. And without that I wouldn't be able to continue the job. The therapist support has been there and that's been invaluable." (Sheila)

Clearly, Access to Work-funded support is central to Sheila's survival at work. It is important to point out that, for some people, survival may be possible with this help, but it does not provide enough support to enable them to thrive. Alan, a worker with cerebral palsy, discussed the provision through Access to Work of a personal assistant (PA) at work:

> "My actual time [with PA support] is limited to 'round about forty to fifty minutes per day, and that is to help me, and put my coat on and make a cup of tea. It's limited, in the sense that I don't get clerical support, yes." (Alan)

This limited provision of PA support meant that he still faced barriers in toileting and completing laborious and time-consuming clerical tasks. Alan felt that with an additional five to six hours per week he would be able to concentrate on the more interesting aspects of his job. Some creative examples of collaborative external support were also provided, for example for Trevor, who got support from his local social services department, Motability (a charity with some statutory funding to provide vehicles and adaptations) and the local Disability Services Team. Trevor

told how his direct payments were linked to these wider supports:

> "Yes, social services [support me], they give me the money to provide my own care, so I can pay for a carer to get me up and get me dressed and in my car in the morning and in the evening.... Well there's Motability – they're helping, they're actually working together with the Disability Service Team to give me a grant towards this vehicle." (Trevor)

Flexible working

A significant number of participants noted how changes to the ordering and location of their work allowed them flexibility. This was particularly important if changes in stamina and/or the need for therapeutic support were evident. Employers and managers were involved in the process (and often the co-funding) of formalised support through Access to Work. Other examples of formal managerial support were given:

> "They're quite good as well if I've got a hospital appointment, even though I only work ten hours they allow me to go in that time and I don't have to pay the hours back. When I have appointments it's always on the day I work and that's because it's the day my consultant's available and they say 'ok, you go off'." (Pauline)

Kate offered an example of managerial flexibility in parking arrangements, which helped to reduce the physical barriers of her workplace. She was allowed to use the rear entrance to her place of work even though other staff were excluded on health and safety grounds:

> "I have had special entrance arrangements made for me, authorised by the area manager, because where I work is quite some distance from the car parking…. It means I haven't got to traipse hundreds of yards from the car park to the main entrance."
> (Kate)

Welfare department support

It is important not to play down the less used forms of support. It could be argued that these sources offer very valuable support but that for whatever reason are not known about or requested. James provided an example of the support offered by his employer's welfare department:

> "I can get help from the welfare officer … the welfare officer will give me advice mainly, or someone you can talk to, to discuss things, perhaps that you couldn't discuss with your line manager. Sometimes it's difficult to talk to your boss." (James)

Other sources of support

Other external agencies were mentioned as providing work support, for example the Shaw Trust and a number of supported employment providers, and there was a creative range of formal support provided to disabled workers. Hopefully, the employment provisions of the 1995 Disability Discrimination Act will add impetus to this provision.

A surprising finding from the research was that there were few examples of support provided by employee welfare departments, personnel specialists or trades unions. This is particularly striking given the strong links previously forged with trades unions organisations by organisations of or for disabled people. The role of these potential sources of support requires further investigation.

It is worth noting that, while many disabled workers did mention their trade union, this was largely in relation to their trade union's information networks on national strategies. One woman talked about her union's local disabled members group and its importance in sharing information about common issues and campaigns. But only in two instances was active union support sought. Anwar found that this took the form of general moral support rather than direct casework advice, and noted that he had three separate grievance submissions (against his employer) sitting in his union's in-tray, two of which had been there "some time". Surprisingly, Anwar was still appreciative of the moral support provided by the local branch, feeling that this was particularly important for him as a disabled employee. Kate, on the other hand, praised her union's advice on her options should she ever need to formalise her concerns about workload.

For Penny, a worker with a learning difficulty, the fact of having work was support in itself:

> "Yes, before I had this job I had no money at all." (Penny)

This is a very chastening comment indeed and reminds us of the relative nature of employment needs. Clearly, the value of work and workplace support only made sense in the context of disabled workers' employment histories, and current expectations about workplace support.

Job redesign or reallocation

The formal redesign or (less commonly) the reallocation of a job or task was seen as a form of support, as it helped focus disabled workers' energies on tasks for which they were more suited. This sometimes happened with the support of Disability Service Teams.

Costs of support

There was evidence that, for a small number of participants, support came with a cost attached. This was usually of a personal, rather than financial kind. Those interviewed were asked about any costs they felt were attached to the support they received, and there were very few reports of cost. Perhaps this is explained by the way in which support develops over time – informal support that comes from colleagues and managers is often not quantified and, while give and take was noted, it was often not expected. Official support was often based on entitlement and would not therefore have obvious costs for the recipient. However, the costs reported do need to be explored so that the financial, emotional or personal costs of support can be distinguished.

Ruth offered a clear picture of the emotional costs of asking for support and adjustments to her daily work:

> "I pay an emotional cost because it is very wearing; it's all very wearing being this firm with

people ... on occasion that leads to some brilliant victories but also on occasion, when you are right, you know the gap between what you have actually managed to get and what you should have got, and that hurts." (Ruth)

She went on to provide an example of the specific costs of asserting her rights to an accessible and inclusive workplace, of a meeting with senior colleagues at which a video presentation was inaccessible to someone with a hearing impairment:

> "I had been on leave and the meeting was in a few minutes time ... I found out accidentally that there was going to be a video shown as part of the meeting ... videos are a pain for me because I can't hear the speech.... I went to see the chief executive ... I said 'how am I going to access the video?' ... the chief executive went 'hmmm' ... I said 'we need a decision. Do you want me to stay in the meeting and look at the ceiling?' ... he said 'don't worry we are not showing it'. Now that required a certain amount of stress on my part." (Ruth)

Joanne made a different point related to a personal cost of support. In order to qualify for employment support she had to accept the definition of being 80% productive. Here, the official cost of support was to accept this 'fact', which she felt was stigmatising. There might arguably be future 'costs' to accepting this point.

> "It rankles a bit that I have to say that I could only do 80% of the job when I set the job up to be honest,

but the financial considerations came first." (Joanne)

Penny, who has a learning difficulty, suggested that the benefits system imposes costs that make a fuller connection with employment very difficult. The 'perverse incentive' at the heart of the benefits system is a clear barrier to Penny seeking the status of a fully-fledged worker.

"I would really like to work longer hours but cannot do so because otherwise I would lose my benefits." (Penny)

Alison reflected on her previous work in which she felt that to ask for support would have had its personal cost:

"... up to that point my needs would have been met with, 'Oh god, she wants something different; she's causing trouble'. So you integrate that into your thinking." (Alison)

The range and depth of support and the often complex links between the different forms of support can be seen in the comments reported in this chapter. The distinction between formal and informal support, although not without problems, proved helpful in terms of informing the research and future ideas of workplace support. It is clear that the quantified forms of external and employer support may not be easily replicated; for example, the extent to which trades unions and the Access to Work programme responded to disabled workers was unpredictable. Being assertive worked in some instances, while in others led to very slow or insubstantial provision. Conversely, some people reported that even tentative enquiries about trades unions and Employment Service support led to swift provision of support, equipment and advice.

Conclusions

This chapter has explored the range of supports that disabled people reported in their workplace. It is clear that both formal and informal support were very important in making workplace survival and thriving possible. Most support was reported to be at little personal or emotional cost. Financial costs did attach to provision under the Access to Work scheme, but this was seen to be outweighed by the benefits of continued support and was often not (directly) obvious to the recipient.

4

Lessons for stakeholders

A number of very useful lessons were gleaned from the research and were addressed to the range of stakeholders identified as important in disabled workers' lives:

- other disabled workers
- colleagues
- employers and managers
- Jobcentre Plus staff.

Summary of stakeholder lessons

Other disabled workers

- Be assertive but not aggressive.
- Accept yourself for who you are.
- Be confident in asking for support.
- Be informed about your rights to support.
- Be open and up-front.

Colleagues

- Don't make assumptions about disabled workers.
- Introduce mandatory disability equality training.
- Be supportive but not overbearing.

Employers and managers

- Disabled people are not a 'special' case for support.
- Ask disabled workers if their needs are being met.
- Be aware of and allow flexible ways of working.
- Encourage mutual respect.
- Be well informed about support options and sources.

Jobcentre Plus staff

- Be better informed about the variety of disabled workers' needs.
- Be consistent and equitable in your provision. Avoid a lottery.
- Be responsive and flexible.
- Share Access to Work recipients' experiences.
- Look at more impartial means of support.

Lessons for other disabled workers

The most commonly noted lessons were those offered by other disabled workers. A common message was that disabled workers should be assertive in expressing their needs and identifying barriers, but should avoid being too strident in their raising of these points. Joanne commented:

"Well, I think if you think back to being younger you are very much more aggressive about being a disabled person, but I don't think that aggression always works because they [employers] see it as a chip on your shoulder." (Joanne)

Alison also discussed the dangers of confrontation about her dyslexia:

"What I am trying to pass on to my friends it's to be careful and to begin a process of self-acceptance, and through that self-acceptance, therefore you move from a lot of positions where you are very dependent on people. But don't put yourself in dangerous situations where if you did come out that it would be a negative experience." (Alison)

Ahmed offered lessons for other disabled people, emphasising confidence and also respect for colleagues:

"... be confident in asking, work hard, think positive, coordinate your time good, and you must respect your colleagues." (Ahmed)

Respect for colleagues and employers could ensure that confidence and assertiveness in acknowledging needs and barriers is presented in a constructive way. This helps to provide a distinction between assertiveness and aggression. Identifying and obtaining appropriate support, both inside and outside of work, was important. Peter talked about the range of support available:

"... I've made sure that I know where things are that might be of help even, if I don't need them now ... where the Access to Work team is based, just let them know you are there as it were ... any local organisations that might be of use. The internal thing – there's no point in being shy about one's situation ... to have the feeling that it's my business and no one else's is quite wrong, because at some stage, one's situation is bound to impact on others and it's better in my view to be up-front...." (Peter)

This comment emphasised the range of support and the need to anticipate future support requirements, as well as being up-front about needs. Pauline made similar points:

"Well, I would say, try and get yourself a broad knowledge of what's out there and what's available, ie direct payments, Access to Work – I didn't know about this when I was at 'ICN'; I'd never heard of it. If I had I could have had an electric wheelchair to whizz around the offices. Try to read [disability] magazines, visit disabled websites...." (Pauline)

The above responses are not necessarily contradictory, but emphasise the need to judge when to be open about asking for support. However, the degree of emphasis on risk given by respondents was quite varied, with comments on 'coming out' when an unseen or previously unknown impairment is acknowledged for the first time. Clearly, needs and barriers are unlikely to be addressed until a disabled worker feels able to declare their disability.

The issue of confidence was central to Alicia:

"Well, I think really that the first thing that is really important is that you are comfortable with who you are and what your limitations are, and to try to be as aware of them as possible. Unless you've got the confidence to go to your employer and say 'look I can work; I can achieve this but you are going to have to be a little flexible with the way that I work and acknowledge that my work is of equal value'. It's about having the negotiating skills really." (Alicia)

This was a more strident appraisal of the qualities needed to obtain understanding and support in the workplace. It moves further towards a more empowered role, being clear and confident not just individually, but also in negotiation about how the reality of disability is presented to others.

Lessons for colleagues

A significant number of messages were offered for colleagues of disabled workers. The question of openness – one already raised by disabled people about their own strategies – was suggested by some participants as being a useful lesson for colleagues too.

"I would say don't make assumptions about people, try to get to know somebody and get to know what they like and what they don't like and what kind of help they want and what kind of help they don't want. And just be open about that really. But also

the issue of trying to create a culture in the workplace where impairment is on the table and is part of how you work together in a supportive way." (Libby)

Caroline also mentioned creating the right environment for inclusion, but felt the need for more structured ways of achieving this:

"Mandatory disability equality training. I suppose the basic stuff like not making assumptions, being prepared to act and listen and the obvious things like treating disabled people as people.... And maybe non-disabled people should be involved in setting up structures to support disabled people in terms of infrastructures at work, like policies and procedures and stuff like that...." (Caroline)

Mike made similar points:

"I think colleagues who are non-disabled need to have an awareness of what it's like to be a blind person, for example, or a deaf person, and have awareness training around those subjects. I also think it helps if people are naturally – I'm trying to think of the right word – it helps if people working in the organisation have a responsible attitude towards people with learning disabilities: not too close and taking over, but at the same time not too distant and keeping aloof." (Mike)

Lessons for employers and managers

Many of the above messages for colleagues could be equally relevant for employers and line managers. Some of the comments that have particular significance for this group are given below. James alluded to the fine balance required between under-support and not being overbearing:

"Just treat them as normal, don't make them a 'special case', just help them if you can, ask them what help they need, you know, or ask if they can manage. Although you can perhaps be too helpful, but obviously, within limits, try and ask them what they need." (James)

Tricia noted how important it was to ask a disabled colleague if there is anything they need, especially when they have an unseen impairment:

"Sometimes just simply asking. I know that might sound a bit silly, but very often, in my case, people aren't aware at all, unless you look awful, that you're either in a lot of pain or feeling faint or something. Just simply asking if somebody could bring something up from downstairs ... just simply passing things, or whatever else, could make the world of difference and no difference to the person that's offering that sort of assistance." (Tricia)

Alicia noted the need for managers to be aware of and accept workplace flexibility:

"I mean, if you are going to work in a flexible way they have to be accepting of that in order that you are going to have a good working relationship with them. I don't think that it is impossible but, again, it comes down to them being aware that there's more than one way of doing something." (Alicia)

Flexibility could also be applied to the acceptance and awareness of a range of impairments. Lyn, a worker with a learning difficulty, commented on this:

"You need to respect each other's needs and to respect the fact we all have different disabilities. I mean, we have, like, we are told about equal opportunities as well, so we have to respect that, and their background and stuff." (Lyn)

A more hands-on solution for conveying messages to managers and employers was suggested by Peter:

"Well, I think employers and supervisors could quite usefully be given a whole set of possibilities, for example [information on] disabled loos, access ramps, rails, signage, Braille signs for people with partial sight, audio facilities.... I think there is a whole range of things employers can be given in a handbook form and encouraged to use, and not so that it gets put on a shelf." (Peter)

Lessons for Jobcentre Plus staff

The other major group identified as in need of information about strategy and support were the Jobcentre Plus disability-related staff (formerly PACTs and now called Disability Service Teams). Some information needs relate to the individual employee, some to policy development of the disability provision offered by Jobcentre Plus.

> "Largely because my experience with the DEAs [disability employment advisors] is that they often don't have sufficient knowledge to work with a wide range of disabled people. That often their communication skills aren't that brilliant. I've also found that quite a lot of them are thrown by the idea that somebody who is disabled having any kind of high-level skills or qualifications.... But I do think there is a lot of work needs to be done, and not just disability employment advisors, but everybody in a Jobcentre needs to have better awareness and better knowledge." (Mary)

Caroline picked up a commonly mentioned point (made by 15 of the 18 Access to Work recipients) that Access to Work provision was experienced as a lottery with no obvious predictors of whether provision would be made, how quickly or how much. This point was also made in the focus group meetings at the end of this research:

> "... it would be nice if we didn't get that kind of postcode lottery-type approach. I mean, it may be inevitable because you get different people in parts of the country doing the job, but if you had a basic understanding of what you were entitled to and how quickly, you'd be able to compare yourself with others and get basically the same treatment regardless of where you live...." (Caroline)

Katherine pointed out the need to provide equipment as a preparation for employment, she noted how a 'catch 22' operates in her area:

> "Well, yeah, I suppose today I need equipment before I even start the job and that's always been a thing, if you want a contract or something, you can't have the equipment until you're fully employed, which is totally silly because you can't do the job without the equipment." (Katherine)

Alison, although a major beneficiary of Access to Work funding, suggested that Jobcentre Plus staff should be more proactive in their role as providers of specialist support:

> "... they have all this contact and possibly asking people [current beneficiaries], to ask if they actually want to go out into other employment situations and talk about their experiences to other [disabled] colleagues and their managers." (Alison)

It was implicit in many responses that participants felt that there was a piece missing from the employment support jigsaw. Although lacking a language with which to describe this unmet need, one message that was offered serves as the concluding comment of this section. It alludes to the need for a vocational advisor who is independent of the employer and the Employment Service:

> "Well, one good thing that I don't have that I wish I had is supervision outside of work, that's not connected to your boss.... She is my boss and she has this power over me and I can't be completely honest. [We need] somebody that's outside of it and someone who can tell you everything, and you can tell them if you've screwed up."
> (Libby)

5

Conclusions and implications for policy and practice

This study has explored the ways in which disabled workers survive or thrive in the workplace. Key areas of interest were the strategies adopted by disabled people to get by or prosper at work. The research also addressed the range of supports that disabled people received which supported their daily working lives.

There is evidence that a wide range of strategies is being adopted, which reduce barriers at work and make employment more successful than it would be otherwise. Strategies range from low-key informal disclosure of impairment through to more direct and formal attempts to address workplace barriers at the beginning of a new job.

Importantly, it would be both inappropriate and, in employment terms, risky to point to any one strategy as the one best way of nurturing workplace success. A range of choices that disabled workers and jobseekers might learn from have been highlighted in this report. One important message from the research is that of an appropriate 'reading' or understanding of an organisation before adopting detailed strategies. Awareness of forms of support, advice and information were also seen as central to disabled workers' workplace successes.

Support was mentioned regularly in the comments of participants. For most workers informal and formal, internal and external forms of support were essential for workplace surviving and thriving. The role of family, friends and disability organisations was significant in increasing the confidence and competence of many of the workers. Working for an organisation of or for disabled people was more likely to allow workplace development for those interviewed.

Colleague support, understanding managers, the government's Access to Work scheme, employment schemes and trades unions were all seen as playing a part in the daily support of most of the disabled workers in this study. Emotional costs of receiving support were mentioned by a small number of participants. The presence of support did not result in a barrier-free workplace and it is important to note that some physical, attitudinal and institutional barriers remained in most of the working environments described by the workers. The need for more coordinated and reliable Access to Work support was frequently mentioned.

Overall, a working environment in which impairments and workplace barriers were openly and sensitively handled was seen by participants to be very important, as was the opportunity to discuss disability issues in a non-judgemental environment. Many individual comments echoed the broader shift in thinking around disability and employment by focusing on ability and diversity instead.

It was clear from the research that unconditional acceptance of workplace diversity and flexibility is at the heart of more enabling workplace regimes. The need for organisations in which disabled workers are not viewed as different or 'outside of the norm' was seen as a prerequisite for future employment success for disabled people.

General policy

There are also a number of implications for policy makers that arise from this research. A significant number of comments were attached to the role and value of the Access to Work scheme. Many positive comments were made about the overall importance of the support the scheme offered. However, a majority of disabled workers who were receiving, or had received, support commented on its length of delivery time, inflexibility, generalist nature and uneven provision. There are also more general policy implications from this research for Jobcentre Plus.

General policy points

- Policy makers need to be aware that much support which is of value to disabled workers is informal or derived from 'custom and practice'. This makes much workplace support

vulnerable to staff turnover. There are also legal implications of founding much workplace support on understanding rather than formal arrangements.
- Policy makers need to be aware that personnel specialists, company welfare officers, equal opportunities staff and trades unions play only a minor role in enhancing disabled workers' strategies and support. The small-scale and infrequent use of these sources indicated that they are seen as a last-ditch option rather than a first port-of-call for the disabled workers researched.
- As a key policy player, the Disability Rights Commission could take a more active educational role and connect more fully with other key employment stakeholders. This would help improve disabled people's employment opportunities.
- Although only a minority viewpoint, some comments related to the need for an informed but impartial vocational support worker. This was especially pertinent for people with mental health problems and learning difficulties. The current relationship between employer, occupational health, Employment Service and welfare/personnel functions could be viewed as outdated. Messages could be taken about a more integrated approach to vocational support.

Department for Work and Pensions: Access to Work

- The Access to Work programme is central to disabled workers' ability to survive and thrive in the workplace.
- Access to Work benefits should extend to pre-employment to help disabled people prepare for work.

- Access to Work should be consistent in its interpretation of eligibility and the appropriate support for disabled applicants.
- Since Access to Work is a national employment scheme, it needs to ensure that benefits are applied equitably across the UK to reduce the sense of it being a 'lottery' of provision. It should be quicker and more responsive to disabled people's needs.

Department for Work and Pensions and the Department of Social Security

- The Department for Work and Pensions, Jobcentre Plus and the Department for Social Security should take note of the evidence in this research that shows that employing disabled people can be a low-cost or no-cost option. These government departments have a key role in disseminating this message and in countering the misconception that it is prohibitively expensive to employ disabled people.
- It is also confirmed by this research that workers with learning difficulties were often unable to combine meaningful working hours with current benefits provisions. There was consistent and compelling evidence to support the need for a more flexible benefits regime.
- The many employment-related policies and initiatives are likely to represent further challenges to joined-up support for disabled workers. The exact relationship between NDDP personal advisors, job brokers, 'Workstep' contract staff and Disability Support Teams is yet to be established. The advent of the 1995 Disability Discrimination Act

may make for even greater challenges in terms of a more holistic approach to job placement, support and retention.

Employers and employers' forums

- Employers, employer and personnel forums should note that disabled workers felt that much more could be done to make colleagues and managers aware of disabled workers' use of strategies and their support needs.
- The 2004 roll-out of the 1995 Disability Discrimination Act requires that small businesses are mainstreamed into the existing employers' forum networks. The Employers Forum on Disability should be encouraged to strengthen their links with the Federation of Small Businesses, Chambers of Commerce and the Small Business Service. Advice, guidance and mentoring support are all likely prerequisites of successfully responding to this expansion of the DDA.
- Organisations of and for disabled people were seen to offer a more supportive environment for the vast majority of workers employed in these organisations. There were clearly some messages and benchmarks of good employer practice that could be imported into general employment policy and practice.

Employee organisations

- Trades unions and their confederations need to be aware that their members viewed their support

as an important but 'last-ditch' option
rather than a first port-of-call.
Further consideration might be given
to the importance of the role and
scope of trades unions in realising
workplace support.

References

Barnes, H., Thornton, P. and Maynard-Campbell, S. (1998) *Disabled people and employment: A review of research and development work*, Bristol/York: The Policy Press/Joseph Rowntree Foundation.

Beinart, S., Smith, P. and Sproston, K. (1996) *The Access to Work programme: A survey of recipients, employers, employment services, managers and staff*, London: Social and Community Planning Research.

Bolderson, H. and Mabbett, D. (2000) 'Policy scenarios for meeting needs without categorisation', Paper presented at the University of Stirling 'What Future for Social Security' Conference, June.

Breakthrough UK (2001) *Landing a job: Working in partnership to employ more disabled people*, Manchester: Breakthrough UK.

Burchardt, T. (2000) *Enduring economic exclusion: Disabled people, income and work*, York: York Publishing Services/Joseph Rowntree Foundation.

Centrica (2001) 'Recruitment that works', Centrica Employers' Forum on Disability and Carers UK.

Daw, R. (2000) *The impact of the Human Rights Act on disabled people*, London: Disability Rights Commission.

DfEE (Department for Education and Employment) (1998) 'New personal advisors service will help disabled people', Press Release, 30 March.

DfEE, DSS (Department of Social Security) and HM Treasury (2001) *Towards full employment in modern society*, Green Paper, London: The Stationery Office.

Disability Now (2002) 'New Deal Probe', September, pp 3-4.

DoH (Department of Health) (2001) *Valuing people: A new strategy for learning disability in the 21st century*, White Paper, London: The Stationery Office.

DRC (Disability Rights Commission) (2002) *Strategic Plan 2001-2004*, London: DRC.

DSS (Department of Social Security) (1999) Welfare Reform and Pensions Bill, London: The Stationery Office.

French, S. (2001) *Disabled people and employment: A study of the working lives of visually impaired physiotherapists*, Aldershot: Ashgate.

Gooding, C. (1995) 'Employment and disabled people: equal rights or positive action', in G. Zarb (ed) *Removing disabling barriers*, London: Policy Studies Institute.

Graham, P., Jordan, A. and Lamb, B. (1990) *An equal chance or no chance?*, London: The Spastics Society.

Griffiths, G. (2001) *Making it work: Inspection of welfare to work for disabled people*, London: Department of Health and the Social Services Inspectorate.

ILO (International Labour Organisation) (2001) *Code of practice on managing disability at the workplace*, Geneva: ILO.

Income Data Services (2000) *Monitoring the Disability Discrimination Act 1995*, Second Report, London: Income Data Services.

Jones, S., Morgan, J., Murphy, D. and Shearn, J. (2002) *Success in supported employment for people with learning difficulties*, Brighton/York: Pavilion Publishing/Joseph Rowntree Foundation.

Lakey, J. and Simpkins, R. (1994) *Employment rehabilitation for disabled people: Identifying the issues*, London: Policy Studies Institute.

Lewis, J. (ed) (2000) *Job retention in the context of long-term illness*, York: Joseph Rowntree Foundation/ Department for Education and Employment.

Martin, J., White, A. and Meltzer, H. (1989) *Disabled adults: Services, transport and employment*, OPCS Surveys of Disability in Britain Report 4, London: HMSO.

O'Bryan, A., Simons, K., Beyer, S. and Grove, B. (2000) *A framework for supported employment*, Policy Consortium for Supported Employment, York: York Publishing Services/Joseph Rowntree Foundation.

RNIB (Royal National Institute for the Blind) (2002) *Work matters: Enabling blind and partially sighted people to gain and retain employment*, London: RNIB.

Roulstone, A. (1998) *Enabling technology: Disabled people, work and new technology*, Buckingham: Open University Press.

Roulstone, A. (2000) 'Disability, New Deal and disabled people', *Disability and Society*, vol 15, no 3, pp 427-45.

Roulstone, A. (2003: forthcoming) 'The legal road to rights? Disabling premises, obiter dicta and the Disability Discrimination Act 1995', *Disability and Society*, vol 18, no 2, pp 117-32.

Sainsbury, R., Corden, A. and Thornton, P. (2001) *Evaluation of the New Deal for Disabled People personal advisor pilot projects*, Report for the Department of Social Security and the Department for Education and Employment, York: Social Policy Research Unit, University of York.

Thomas, A. (1992) *Working with a disability: Barriers and facilitators*, London: Social and Community Planning Research.

Zadek, S. and Scott-Parker, S. (2001) *Unlocking potential: Disability and the business case*, London: Employers' Forum on Disability.

Appendix: Research methods

Phase 1

Recruiting participants

In order to maximise the number and spread of people taking part in the research, the project was widely advertised, using established sources such as disability newspapers and organisations, as well as a range of existing networks used by disabled people. Recommendations for distribution of this 'call for participants' were also made by the Project Advisory Group (PAG) members. Potential participants were invited to register an initial interest in taking part in the research and request the questionnaire in a format accessible to them. An advertisement and flyer were developed and used as an initial contact with all sources.

Attracting disabled people who were not necessarily linked to established networks or the disabled people's 'movement' was important. Outlets for the advertisement and flyer included newspapers, newsletters, mailing lists of organisations, personal contacts, email sources, the Internet and service providers (such as British Sign Language [BSL] interpreters).

It was also recognised as essential to include people with learning difficulties and Deaf people. People First, CHANGE, the British Deaf Association and known BSL interpreters were contacted to seek publicity and contacts. The project was also publicised at the Employment Conference in Derby, which many Deaf people attended. A number of people (having seen the advertisement or flyer) also publicised the project within their own networks.

Developing the initial questionnaire

The questionnaire was developed with a code for responses and analysis. The questionnaire was split into sections:

- contact details
- employment details
- strategy and support details, that is support at work, support outside work (family and friends), personal assistance and organisations (Jobcentre Plus, organisation of disabled people, trade unions and so on)
- information about the disabled individual, including age, gender, sexual identity, ethnic origin and impairment.

The final section was included in order that a wide range of disabled people in different circumstances could participate in the study. It was also recognised that experiencing different sorts of discrimination might play a part in the development of individuals' strategies and use of support. The draft questionnaire was piloted to eliminate potential problems. After the pilot, the questionnaire was made available in a range of accessible formats.

Although efforts were made to keep the questionnaire as straightforward as possible, it became apparent that an 'easy words' version would need to be developed separately for people with learning difficulties. This was undertaken by the organisation CHANGE.

Responses to the initial questionnaire

A total of 332 questionnaires were distributed in the following formats:

- standard print (14-point font) – 191
- large print (18-point font) – 8
- Braille – 11
- audio tape – 5
- computer disk – 8
- email – 70
- 'easy words' – 39

A total of 167 completed questionnaires were returned. The employment, strategy and monitoring details (age, gender, geographical location) of these respondents were recorded. Nine questionnaires were considered invalid due to participants being in voluntary work or retired. A number of completed questionnaires were also sent back too late for inclusion in the Phase 1 analysis and selection of the main sample. In total, 156 questionnaires were valid for

the purposes of the research; of the 156 valid questionnaires analysed, 91 (58%) were women and 65 (42%) were men.

Pilot and Phase 2

Participants from Phase 1 were then selected and invited to take part in Phase 2. The factors affecting selection included:

- geographical location (to ensure, as far as possible, that all areas were represented)
- length of employment (minimum of two years' working experience)
- equality/personal profile issues (age, gender, ethnicity, sexual identity)
- type of work
- position within business/organisation
- number of hours worked
- types of strategies used
- types of support reported
- impairment type.

Care was taken to ensure that a diversity of impairments were included in the Phase 2 participants. This was important when deciding whether people were interviewed by telephone or face to face. People with learning difficulties, speech impairments and D/deaf people were all offered face-to-face interviews.

An interview schedule was developed, based on the initial questionnaire, which sought to ensure that the information already provided was built on and expanded. The schedule was piloted with five respondents to ensure the interview was accessible and appropriate. Relatively few changes were made to the interview schedule following the pilot interviews.

A total of 47 participants were invited to take part in Phase 2 of the project. Of these, 33 eventually formed the main Phase 2 group (18 women [52%] and 15 men [48%]). They provided an illustrative sample based on key variables identified by the researchers as important for the research.

The process of interviewing the main sample of participants was given careful thought and attention. The 47 people were contacted by letter (or email) and asked whether they were still interested in participating, and if so, whether they wished the interview to be conducted by telephone or face to face. There was a small 'fall-out' of respondents at this stage, mainly due to changes in their lives, but not enough to prejudice the main sample.

All interviews were taped, with the permission of the participants and transcribed verbatim. Transcribers were used who would be able to work positively with the tapes of interviewees with speech impairments or using BSL interpreters. Guidelines were given to the selected transcribers to ensure consistent transcriptions were provided.

The majority of in-depth (Phase 2) interviews were conducted by telephone, with nine face-to-face interviews for better access.

Coding of the transcriptions of interviews was carried out according to a framework devised early in the research and revised following the pilot interviews. Detailed interpretation of data was possible from the qualitative analysis. Initial broad assessment of the 33 interviews carried out confirmed that the items identified within the coding framework were useful

and relevant as headings for interpreting disabled people's experiences.

The coding framework aimed to distinguish between support (described to participants as 'things you get to help you at work') and strategies ('what you devise to help you survive [get by] and thrive [get on] in work'). The analysis used illustrative quotes from the taped interviews.

Coding of strategies used experiences of present and past jobs and before starting work. Coding mapped both strategies internal and external to the work setting, including those relating to:

- managers/supervisors
- colleagues/workmates
- the employing organisation
- trades unions
- friends/family/partner
- organisations *of* disabled people
- organisations *for* disabled people
- social services
- Jobcentre Plus/Access to Work
- finance/benefits
- environment/equipment.

Coding of support covered the same range of issues and also included identification of the source of the support.

Defining 'strategy' and 'support'

Following the pilot interviews, definition of 'strategies' and 'support' became a major factor. After discussion within the team and the Project Advisory Group, it was agreed that the following definitions would be used in interviews.

Strategies came from the individual disabled person. They involved thinking through options, making decisions and choices, planning ahead, working out the best ways to get by and get on, testing out different approaches, working out how to tackle disablism in the workplace, and taking action to get the support needed. There was a conscious (or sometimes subconscious) process that came from the individual.

Supports came from outside the individual – from a colleague, a scheme, financial allowances or benefits, changes to the environment or job structure, and so on. They could be emotional, moral, practical, financial, technical, environmental, or organisational. Some of these supports would be provided without the individual having to request them (and therefore they would not require the individual to develop any strategy to access them). There would also be supports that were already in place, or were put in place, that people felt made the experience of work and the workplace better and that did not require any thinking or action by the disabled person. In contrast, there would be other supports that required a lot of 'strategy' (thinking and action) if the individual was to succeed in accessing them.

'Support' was therefore taken to include internal and external forms of advice, help, adjustments and flexibilities; these then included the informal role of family and friends and the usually formalised role of trades unions, disability/disabled people's organisations and the Employment Service. Colleagues, line managers and employers clearly could provide both formal and informal support. Likewise, 'strategies' were seen as coming from a number of sources, or were channelled through these different routes. Efforts were made to put current employment strategies and support into a longer timeframe with interview

discussion of previous employment and the longer-run development of strategies where appropriate. These refined definitions helped us to build a coding framework that more accurately reflected the complexity of the relationship between strategies and support.

Phase 3

Focus groups

The final phase of the study involved holding two focus groups: one in Manchester and the other in London. Everyone who had taken part in Phase 2 was invited to attend a focus group. The groups were facilitated by two members of the research team and the discussions focused on:

- feedback on the research findings
- ways of disseminating the research findings to other disabled people, employers, colleagues and Jobcentre Plus staff.

Although only eight participants were able to attend the focus group meetings (five in London and three in Manchester), the meetings proved valuable in confirming the wider research findings and inferences.